This superb collection of cartoons by Pont, one of the most eminent pre-war Punch artists contains many of his most famous cartoons and shows that his genius for captivating the idiosyncrasies and lunacies of the British is still accurate, alive and amusing today. New readers will undoubtedly indulge in a strongly British characteristic — laughing at themselves.

*"Pont is undeniably a genius . . . to examine Pont's toweringly brilliant work, we must ignore all those commentators who down the years have insisted on describing him as a penetrating social observer. He was nothing of the kind; he was a collector of clichés. He was the easel equivalent of Saki and Wodehouse".* ALAN COREN

# THE BRITISH CHARACTER

*" . . . and of course he'll go into his
father's business, when he grows up."*

# THE
# BRITISH
# CHARACTER

STUDIED AND REVEALED

BY

PONT

WITH AN INTRODUCTION

BY

ALAN COREN

*A Nadder Book*
ELEMENT BOOKS LTD

First published by Collins 1938

Reprinted many times

A Nadder Book
This Edition published by Element Books Ltd 1982

Cover design by Humphrey Stone

Printed and bound in Great Britain by
Robert Hartnoll Ltd Bodmin Cornwall

ISBN 0 906540 23 2

# CONTENTS

THE ILLUSTRATIONS IN THIS BOOK
ARE REPRODUCED FROM 'PUNCH'
BY PERMISSION OF THE PROPRIETORS

# INTRODUCTION
*by*
## ALAN COREN

JODHPURED, tweeded, souped-and-fished, collars
detached and stockings lisle, bowlered, spatted, feet
brogued and hunting-booted, caped, furred and
solar-topeed, the British characters of Pont honk
and bumble their idiosyncratic way through that
curious limbo-land called caricature, suspended not
between life and death, but between life and fantasy.

Were they ever, even during the flowering of the
Metroland Age d'Or half a century ago, truly alive?
Were nannies bloodthirsty, housewives dumb, and
men exclusively obsessed by golf and hunting? Were
all our parents tone-deaf, xenophobic, venal,
Philistine? Was tea their major passion, with bridge
and dogs close on its heels, and did it always rain?

Of course not, is the short answer. The other
short answer is yes, of course. That is the way it is
with social caricature. Cultural clichés were manu-
factured, once, from truth; that is why they are
now clichés. But what have clichés to do with art,
which, if it is about anything, is about fresh
perception? That is the central question of Pont to
which we ought to address ourselves, if we choose
to engage in the fraught and murky business of
Addressing Ourselves to Central Questions. For
Pont is undeniably a genius who, equally un-

deniably, dealt exclusively in cliché. To examine Pont's toweringly brilliant work, we must ignore all those commentators who down the years since his sad early death at 32 in 1940 have insisted on describing him as a penetrating social observer. He was nothing of the kind; he was a collector and enshriner of clichés. He was the easel equivalent of Saki and Wodehouse, and that is not a bad equivalent to be, at all.

Examine the sub-headings in *The British Character: Enthusiasm for hunting; Fondness for cricket; Absence of the gift of conversation; A weakness for old beams; Love of being horsey; Importance of not being intellectual; Love of writing letters to The Times; Enjoyment of club life; Importance of breeding* . . . not only do they not represent (remember he began drawing them in 1934, in the depths of the Depression) the British character, they do not even represent the character of the narrow class with which Pont was preoccupied: all they represent is a *selection* of characteristics which had themselves been European clichés for a hundred years, largely through Punch's continuing tradition of gently self-knocking silliness. They were doubtless responsible for the fact that German agents were dropped into England wearing bowler hats and plus-fours, and that Goebbels seriously believed that dear old P. G. Wodehouse was a wonderful prize as a social commentator whose every syllable from Occupied France would be accepted *ex cathedra*.

I mention Wodehouse yet again for, I think, good reason: because Pont's genius, like his, lay in manufacturing an entirely self-contained world of English comic fantasy: a colonial four, in evening dress, plays bridge in an African clearing, a dining-car breakfasts angrily in a tornado of chilling air, a group of horsey fools roar around a rural fireside in company with their horses, a tropical-kitted golfer sits on the shoulders of his black bearer and tees off from a jungle lily-pad. But in all these loony land-scapes, there are two glitteringly hard realities: the faces, the figures, the gestures, the manners are real, are true, are observed with a shrewdness and clarity and subtlety which is no part of the cliché and the fantasy of their imagined circumstances. And the other reality is that the line is superb.

The genius is all in the eye and the hand. Pont is an artist. Odd how one never associates artistic genius with the British character.

"*Now, I want you to be particularly brave about the next part.*"

# FOREWORD
## to the original edition

A BOOK of drawings, composed of nothing but drawings, will lie upon the tables of the booksellers, thumbed but unsold until Doomsday. The customers will pick it up, but after they have looked at the drawings the customers will put the book back on the table and spend the precious shillings on SOMETHING TO READ. My agent told me this and the publisher said it was so, so there can be no doubt about it at all.

"A high standard of literary ability will not be expected in the artist," said the agent, kindly but pointedly. So the artist, with a heavy heart, hired a typewriter at half a crown a week, and in the intervals of watching the seasons change beyond the window, produced the six literary effects which will be found scattered about this book. It is hoped that these effects, rising before the eyes of possible purchasers in the form of visions of printed words, will have the result that the agent and the publisher expect.

*Pont.*

# BREEDING

" *It's* **YOUTH** *you need in a business like yours, Mr. Zinkbaum.
Youth, with its imagination, drive and enthusiasm.*"

*" We all have to make mistakes
sometimes, Miss Heslop."*

THE BRITISH CHARACTER.
IMPORTANCE OF BREEDING.

# THE SOCIAL SYSTEM

THE British, with their tidy minds,
Divide themselves up into kinds.
The common kind they call the masses,
The better kind—the upper classes.
In either case it's really not
A specially inspiring lot.
The common ones play darts in pubs,
The others slowly die in clubs.

THE BRITISH CHARACTER.
ENJOYMENT OF CLUB LIFE.

THE BRITISH CHARACTER.
TENDENCY NOT TO KNOW WHAT TO DO ON
SUNDAYS.

# NUMBER TEN DOWNING STREET

THE Prime Minister was busy in his study
Attending to some very serious things,
When suddenly the telephone on table
Gives off a most disturbing lot of rings.

The statesmen for a moment is quite flustered,
And can't think what it is he ought to do,
But finally he picks up the receiver
And says: "Hallo there! What's that? Oh! It's *you*!"

"Why, yes," he says in answer to some question,
"I'm Prime Minister of England all right,
Yes, I'm the man who guides the British people
And steers their ship of something through the night."

But after that his manner seems to alter,
He has the air of some one quite upset;
He says, "I really cannot answer that one,
And I'm not prepared to discuss National Debt.

"It isn't in the interests of the Nation
So it's really not the slightest bit of good
Your asking me to answer all those questions—"
And rings off muttering, "Couldn't, if I would."

## THE BRITISH CHARACTER.
### POLITICAL APATHY.

"*To be perfectly frank, my dear lady, no, I can't hear a 'funny humming noise.'*"

## THE BRITISH CHARACTER.
### PRONENESS TO SUPERSTITION.

THE BRITISH CHARACTER.

A TENDENCY TO THINK THINGS NOT SO GOOD AS THEY USED
TO BE.

# THE ARTS

*" ' Once more into the breach, dear friends,*
*once more . . .' "*

## THE BRITISH CHARACTER.
### Tendency to learn the piano when young.

## THE BRITISH CHARACTER.
### Failure to Appreciate good Music.

## THE BRITISH CHARACTER.
### Love of Detective Fiction.

. . . " *This looks to me like ' Dead-Face ' Anderson's work,*" *gasped Derective- Inspector Watkins, eyeing the corpse in the bath.* . . ."

THE BRITISH CHARACTER.
LOVE OF ARRIVING LATE AT THEATRICAL PRODUCTIONS.

## THE BRITISH CHARACTER.
### PATIENCE.

## THE BRITISH CHARACTER.
### THE GIFT FOR WATER COLOURS.

# THE EMPIRE SPIRIT

# LINES

FROM Afric's steaming Jungles
    To India's arid Plains
The Natives are dependent
    Upon the White Man's Brains.

It is the White Man's Duty,
    As everybody knows,
To teach the black to feel ashamed
    And then to sell him cloes.

Instead of letting him exist
    Just how and where he pleases,
We teach him how to live like Us
    And die of Our Diseases.

We move him from his valleys
    To airy mountain-tops
Where he won't undermine his health
    By raising herds and crops.

The most disturbing nightmare
    Which haunts each White Man's son
Is: "If there had been no White Men
    What *would* the Blacks have done?"

# THE BRITISH CHARACTER.
## Aptitude for Building Empires.

THE BRITISH CHARACTER.
REFUSAL TO ADMIT DEFEAT.

## THE BRITISH CHARACTER.
### IMPORTANCE OF NOT BEING AN ALIEN.

THE BRITISH CHARACTER.
ADAPTABILITY TO FOREIGN CONDITIONS.

THE BRITISH CHARACTER.

IMPERIALISM.

*" Of course we must face facts.*
*It's going to mean waiting."*

THE BRITISH CHARACTER.
LOVE OF KEEPING CALM.

*" There are times when I really begin to
wonder if all this is worth while."*

# LOVE OF ANIMALS

*" What about you and me and
a little home ?"*

*" Sometimes I think they understand
every word we say!"*

## THE BRITISH CHARACTER.
### STRONG TENDENCY TO BECOME DOGGY.

THE BRITISH CHARACTER.
LOVE OF DUMB ANIMALS.

## THE BRITISH CHARACTER.
### LOVE OF WRITING LETTERS TO 'THE TIMES.'

# DOMESTIC

*" And, now, will you open it or shall I?"*

"*There will be nineteen extra to lunch to-day.*"

## THE BRITISH CHARACTER.
### ABSENCE OF IDEAS FOR MEALS.

*. . . then pour the boiling water out
of the kettle into the teapot.*

## THE BRITISH CHARACTER.
### ABSENCE OF THE GIFT FOR COOKING.

## short story in the new manner

. . . the old carpet sweeper . . . three pieces . . . all in
bits . . . what on earth did we ever buy that for . . . if
i shut my eyes i can see kingscrossstation . . . i wonder
why that is . . . somebody told me once . . . i must
think . . . no time to think . . . through the trapdoor
i can see janet with the featherduster but if i shut my
eyes i can see kingscrossstation . . . hullo janet *there* you
are . . . hullo mum there *you* are . . . now then janet
ive spokentoyouaboutthatbefore . . . let us throw all
these things out of the skylight . . . but not that or
these and certainly not that i bought it the year freddie
felldownthestairs mrs henry tuddy . . . mrs henry tuddy
. . . oh yes i remember now the woman with the arms
. . . if i shut my eyes now i can see mrs tuddys arms
. . . what exceptionally fine arms mrs tuddy had . . .
the boxes might come in useful janet . . . i said the
boxes might come in yes in . . . idiot the girl is . . . i
wonder what she did to have suchveryfinearms . . . no
janet i said these things in this trunk look like something-
orother palms . . . palms . . . PALMS . . . why mum
they look more to me like your old fur coat . . . that is
exactly what they are janet . . . dear mrs tuddy . . . i
have been wondering all day . . .

THE BRITISH CHARACTER.
LOVE OF NEVER THROWING ANYTHING AWAY.

*" Don't trouble, George, dear, I can
manage quite well without it."*

THE BRITISH CHARACTER.

A TENDENCY TO PUT THINGS AWAY SAFELY.

## THE BRITISH CHARACTER.
### ABSENCE OF ENTHUSIASM FOR ANSWERING LETTERS.

## THE BRITISH CHARACTER.
### THE EXALTATION OF CLEANLINESS.

"*I expect that was to-day's I was
lighting the fire with, sir.*"

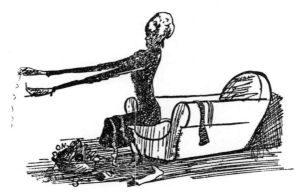

"*It's quite all right, dear, I can manage
perfectly well without them—honestly I
can,*"

"*I've just been wondering, dear, if I don't prefer the piano in the upstairs room after all.*"

# SOCIAL SENSE

*" Well, and what can you talk about?"*

THE BRITISH CHARACTER.
ATTITUDE TOWARDS HOSTESSES.

*" I was just saying, darling, that I see*
*Clark Gable is on to-night."*

THE BRITISH CHARACTER.
A TENDENCY NOT TO JOIN THE LADIES.

# MENU

*Luncheon.*

Broth de l'Ecosse

Filet de Sole Fried

Bœuf Roti avec Pudding de Yorkshire
Pommes de Terre Baked
Sprouts de Brussels

Pomme Tart et Whipped Cream

Café 6d. extra

THE BRITISH CHARACTER.
LOVE OF EVERYTHING FRENCH.

" . . . *and the doctors* all *said they'd* never *seen one like it.*"

THE BRITISH CHARACTER.

ABSENCE OF THE GIFT OF CONVERSATION.

# WILD DUCK

I REMEMBER a little incident that occurred when I was a young man. I was very young and quite ingigulous, don't you know. It didn't strike me as being at all funny at the time, but I must admit that since then I have had many a good laugh about it. Ha! Ha! It happened that one afternoon I was on my way to a friend's house. I must explain that he had invited me; sent a message in fact. And also that at one time he was considered by Lord Hippleton to be the finest Tramusher of his day, but so far as I know nobody plays the game nowadays.

Well, anyway, he became chief assistant commissioner at Rangoon eventually, and a very fine show he put up too. "Old Jithers" we always called him. Ask any one who knew Rangoon in those days and they'll say the same thing: "Splendid job old Pipeye did." Ten minutes it used to take, but things have changed a lot since then. I haven't been near North Africa for years so I can't say. And what do you think I found when I got there? I don't expect you'll guess, very few do, so I'll tell you. There, lying on the floor of the Tramcar was a brace of Wild Duck!

## THE BRITISH CHARACTER.
### FONDNESS FOR LAUGHING AT OUR OWN ANECDOTES.

## THE BRITISH CHARACTER.
### PARTIALITY FOR OPEN FIRES.

*" Gosh!  Quails in Aspic again."*

*" Tell me, are you a believer in elemental disproportion or de-energised statics, or do you just stick to the Propkoffer theory ? "*

## THE BRITISH CHARACTER.
### IMPORTANCE OF NOT BEING INTELLECTUAL.

## THE BRITISH CHARACTER.
### A TENDENCY TO BE HEARTY.

# RURAL

"*Precisely the same as they said about poor Frederic, my dear, and he scarcely lasted the week.*"

## THE BRITISH CHARACTER.
### EXTRAORDINARY PROPENSITY OF THE FARMERS TO GRUMBLE

*" He says it's not for sale, my lord."*

PONT

## THE BRITISH CHARACTER.
### Determination Not to Preserve the Rural Amenities.

## THE BRITISH CHARACTER.
### IMPORTANCE OF TEA.

## THE BRITISH CHARACTER.
### Enthusiasm for Gardening.

*" Look who's come to see baby!"*

THE BRITISH CHARACTER.
A WEAKNESS FOR OAK BEAMS.

THE BRITISH CHARACTER.
KEEN INTEREST IN THE WEATHER.

THE BRITISH CHARACTER.
Passion for the Antique.

# TRAVEL

*" When I was a young man I wasn't
perpetually rushing about in motor cars."*

*" And do I have to keep on holding this?"*

## THE BRITISH CHARACTER.
### PREFERENCE FOR DRIVING ON THE CROWN OF THE ROAD.

THE BRITISH CHARACTER.
TENDENCY TO BE EMBARRASSED BY FOREIGN CURRENCIES.

## THE BRITISH CHARACTER.
### Fondness for Travel.

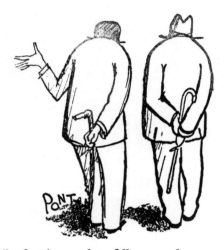

" *The fact is, my dear fellow—and you may as well admit it—we're not so young as we were forty years ago.*"

## THE BRITISH CHARACTER.
### RESERVE.

THE BRITISH CHARACTER.
LOVE OF TRAVELLING ALONE.

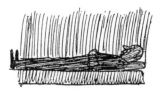

*" Don't be so silly, darling. Would Mother be
likely to say it did if it didn't?"*

*"And now Mother's very cross indeed
with you!"*

## THE BRITISH CHARACTER.
### The Attitude Towards Fresh Air.

*" No, you can't marry Greta Garbo until you grow up, so stop being a baby about it."*

## THE BRITISH CHARACTER.
### The Sea Sense.

## THE BRITISH CHARACTER.
### IMPORTANCE OF EXERCISE.

# SPORT

*" Come on, every one, let's have a race out
to the raft."*

*" It seems ridiculous that by this time nobody*
*has thought of an easier way to do these."*

THE BRITISH CHARACTER.
LOVE OF OPEN-AIR SPORTS.

## THE BRITISH CHARACTER.
### FONDNESS FOR CRICKET.

## THE BRITISH CHARACTER.
### IMPORTANCE OF BEING ATHLETIC.

" *I wonder if there's a really* nice *little boy in
the room who would like to run upstairs and
look for Mummy's spectacles.*"

## THE BRITISH CHARACTER.
### INDISPENSABILITY OF GOLF.

## THE BRITISH CHARACTER.
### LOVE OF GAMES.

## THE BRITISH CHARACTER.
### Enthusiasm for Hunting.

## THE BRITISH CHARACTER.
### LOVE OF BEING HORSEY.

SOME PEOPLE
ARE
NEVER
SATISFIED.